DOODLE JOURNEYS

STEP OUTSIDE.
TAKE THIS BOOK.
ADVENTURE
AWAITS.

DOODLE JOURNEYS

A FILL-IN JOURNAL FOR EVERYDAY EXPLORERS

Dawn DeVries Sokol

Amulet Books
NEW YORK

Cataloging-in-Publication Data has been applied for and may be obtained by the Library of Congress.

Text and illustrations copyright © 2018 Dawn DeVries Sokol

ISBN: 978-1-4197-2862-4

Printed and bound in China
10 9 8 7 6 5 4 3 2 1

Amulet Books are available at special discounts when purchased in quantity for premiums and promotions as well as fundraising or educational use. Special editions can also be created to specification. For details, contact specialsales@abramsbooks.com or the address below.

ABRAMS The Art of Books
195 Broadway, New York, NY 10007
abramsbooks.com

tHiS BOOK BELONGS to:

_____

CONTENTS

INTRODUCTION

"ARE WE THERE YET?"

Usually asked from the backseat of a car, this question implies that it is the destination, not the journey, that is more important. But that couldn't be further from the truth.

Part of the adventure is the actual process of getting there—whether it is by car, plane, boat, or train, we need to appreciate the actual journey itself.

When you take this book with you—anywhere—you will discover new and interesting aspects of a trip that maybe you weren't aware of before. Every time you step out your front door, a journey awaits you. "Travel" is not limited to vacations overseas or a cross-country road trip. Even everyday jaunts to the grocery store, the park, or the dentist can be filled with elements typically gone unnoticed. It's fun to document those through doodles, collage, and words to create a record of where you've been and where you'll be going.

Using this book will allow you to see and think differently about the world around you. The more we see, the more we learn about others and ourselves.

So take it in. Jot it down. Doodle it, cut and paste it, color it in. It's a big wide world out there, and it's yours for the taking!

HOW to USE THIS BOOK

1 As with all of my doodle books, I encourage you to flip through this one and create in the spaces that feel right to you. You don't have to start at the beginning and go through each prompt one after the other. You can work on several prompts at once, jumping back and forth between them if you want. I like to play on several pages at the same time in my journals.

2 This book isn't meant to be a record of one trip or one vacation. There are many journeys for you to take in here. It's time to see yourself as an everyday adventurer.

3 Chapter One is filled with exercises to get you doodling and creating. Use this chapter any time you aren't feeling inspired or you just need a nudge.

4 Chapter Two encourages you to take imaginary trips, which will spark even more creativity than you dreamed! Play in this section whenever you want to take a mental vacation.

5 Chapter Three guides us on real journeys—local and distant. Through imaginary jaunts and exercising our creative muscles, we will learn to take actual trips like pros!

THE TRAVEL

Traveling with art supplies doesn't have to be difficult. You'll be justly equipped with only a ballpoint pen or ordinary pencil in your pocket. But if you want to have a few options for mark-making tools and such, here's what I suggest having on hand:

PENS

BLACK FINE-TIP PENS

Sakura Pigma Micron pens use archival quality ink and have

several size tips, such as .01, .03, and .05. The smaller the number, the smaller the tip. For a thicker tip, try the .08.

GEL PENS

I love to carry a few gel pens because they add great color

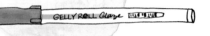

to journal pages and allow for bright doodles. Any Sakura gel pen will work well. Gelly Roll Glaze pens dry clear and jewel-toned, whereas the Soufflé pens are pastel and not as shiny once the ink dries. Other Sakura gel pens include the Gelly Roll Moonlights (which are neon), Gelly Roll

TOOLKit

Stardust (which are glittery), and Gelly Roll Metallic. All offer options for adding color to your doodles and are readily available in craft stores.

MARKERS

Crayola Pip-Squeaks Markers are widely available, come in many colors, and are a fun, inexpensive marker option. Plus, they're small enough to carry with you.

PENCILS

COLORED PENCILS

Any colored pencil will do! I like to use watercolor pencils— you can use them like a regular colored pencil or wet the tip of your finger and slightly rub the color on the page to smear it like paint!

STABILO 3-IN-1 PENCILS

These chunky colored pencils come in 18 colors and function as a colored pencil, watercolor, and wax crayon in one. The extra-thick lead works on many smooth surfaces and is great for painting, too!

NO. 2 PENCIL

The No. 2 is tried and true! Just don't use the eraser too much.
It's best to just keep doodling—don't interrupt the flow by stopping to erase.

CRAYONS

Regular crayons, such as Crayola, lend a textured
look to your doodles. You can also use Crayola Oil Pastels
with a lighter hand, but make sure to smear them into the page;
otherwise they may rub off onto the facing page.

ATTACHMENTS

There are so many ways to attach pictures and collage bits to your pages:

GLUE STICKS

UHU Stic or Elmer's Glue Sticks both work
well and are a less messy option than
regular glue. Both can be found in any
craft or art supply store.

TOMBOW MONO ADHESIVE

My personal favorite for gluing bits of collage is Tombow MONO Adhesive, which can be found at craft stores. The adhesive is applied by a tape roller, and it's easy to take with you for moments of sudden inspiration.

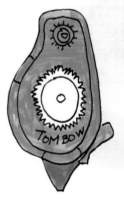

 ## PAPER CLIPS

Paper clips are a great way to attach items to your pages and add some extra flair, since they come in all shapes and colors!

PHOTO CORNERS

A cool, decorative way to add a photo to your book.

STICKERS

So many stickers, so little time! Stickers are a great way to add your personal touch to your pages. You can also use them to attach bits and photos to your book pages.

TAPES

Washi tape, duct tape, masking tape, Scotch tape—ANY kind will do! Use tape to line the edges of your photos or collage bits. Scotch tape may darken over time, but it will look cool in years to come. It's easy to get a little carried away with all the cool tapes out there. Try to keep it to one or two when you're traveling to save room for other tools, too!

SCISSORS

It's a good idea to carry a tiny pair of scissors with you for cutting images and shapes out of pictures and magazine pages. The tiny size makes it easy to cut out small items.

COLLAGE BiTS

Throughout this book, I mention using collage bits. While you are "traveling," collect various papers, ribbons, stamps, receipts, candy wrappers, and flat things you find on the ground (nothing disgusting!). As long as it lies flat, you can easily add it to your book. Before I go, I like to make a little collection of things I already have and then add to it during my adventures.

You will soon be going on a fun road trip with friends or family.

CAMERA

It's great if you have access to a camera while you are exploring. You can document your adventures with a photo when doodles and words alone just won't do!

PHOTO PRINTER

Of course, if you have a camera with you, it's nice to have a litte photo printer in with your supplies, too. There are several kinds out there that will connect with your phone or digital camera. It's NOT a must, though. You can easily print photos when you get home and finish documenting there.

PEN POUCH

I like to gather my tools and collage bits in a pen pouch or case—one that isn't much bigger than this book. That way you don't take too much with you. Choose tools you like best, and keep them to a number you can fit into your case. Pick a few colors each of markers and/or crayons—you don't need to take the whole set. Of course, a small resealable plastic storage bag works well, too. It will seal well and also be see-through so you can easily find what you're looking for.

"IT'S NOT THE DESTINATION — IT'S THE JOURNEY."

—Anonymous

CHAPTER 1

DOODLE DRILLS

FOR THE WANDERLUST SPIRIT

Let's create our way into adventure with some exercises to get your artistic mind moving. Once you find your mojo, jump to whichever prompts in the book interest you. Then, whenever you need a little nudge, come back to this section to pump you up.

TAKE YOUR PENCIL FOR A WALK.

Move your pencil around on these pages and don't think about drawing anything in particular. Just let your mind wander with your pencil. (NO erasing!)

TRY TO KEEP YOUR PENCIL
MOVING WITHOUT TAKING IT
OFF THE PAGE.

UNFAMILIAR

TERRITORY

Draw a picture with your nondominant hand! (If you ordinarily use your right hand, draw with your left instead and vice versa.) It feels weird at first but will loosen you up!

GO-to

STUCK? TRY DRAWING STARS,
CARS, TRAINS, PLANES, OR
CLOUDS!

DOODLES ||||||||

What are the doodles
you return to again and
again? Draw them here.

TRAVEL BLIND

Close your eyes and let your pencil or pen roam on these pages. Now, open your eyes. Do you spot any shapes? Color them in and add to them.

25

What do you bring with you when you travel? Doodle those things here.

THINK OF DESTINATIONS, SUCH AS
SCHOOL, CAMPING, OR A TRIP WITH YOUR
FAMILY. WHAT DO YOU TAKE ON EACH OF
THESE ADVENTURES? LABEL YOUR LISTS
IF YOU MAKE MORE THAN ONE.

Doodle around the shapes on the page to create a scene.

29

ALPHABET

Collage and/or doodle a city out of letters.

city

CUT LETTERS AND OTHER BITS OUT
OF MAGAZINES AND USE THEM TO
BUILD SKYSCRAPERS AND LANDMARKS.
DOODLE OVER THE LETTERS TO JOIN
STRUCTURES TOGETHER.

Draw around the photos on the next few pages to create a scene, people, or animals.

PHOTO FINDS

BE LITERAL OR USE YOUR IMAGINATION! ADD A HUMAN BODY TO THE BIRD HEAD, OR TURN THE ROSE ABOVE INTO A HAT FOR SOMEONE! MAKE THE ELEPHANT ON THE NEXT PAGE INTO A DIFFERENT CREATURE!

STAMP STUDY

Design your own postage stamps!

UNSURE OF WHAT TO DOODLE?
USE THE POSTAGE STAMPS
HERE AS INSPIRATION!

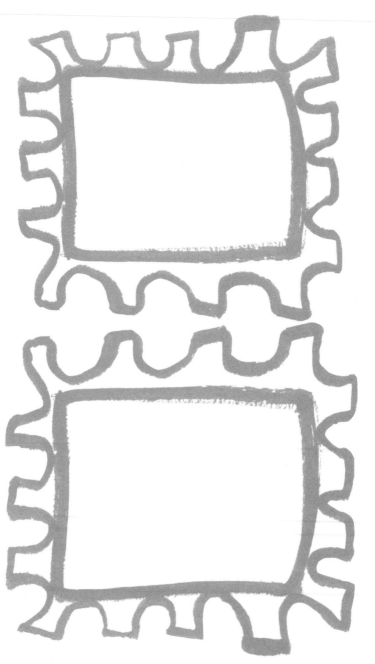

URBAN CIRCLE

Think about a city you know. It can be one you've seen in a movie or the one you live in! Try to draw it using circles only.

Spend the day collecting scraps of paper on your journeys.
Cut out shapes from these papers and paste them down on
these pages. Doodle around them to create your own scene.

POSTAGE

ANYTHING IS POSSIBLE—
A QUEEN WITH A MERMAID
BODY IS A START!

PEOPLE

Finish doodling the people featured in the postage stamps.

WORLD OF SQUARES

Think about the places you visited today.
Draw one of them using only squares.

DRAW YOUR OWN
PICTURE FROM THE
DOODLE STARTED HERE!

JOURNEY WHEREVER
IMAGINATION TAKES
YOU — TO THE MOON
AND THE STARS,
TO ANOTHER TIME
OR PLACE IN
YOUR DREAMS.

CHAPTER 2

IMAGINARY TRIPS

FOR THE CREATIVE MIND

Time to take an adventure in our minds—
consider it a staycation for the brain! Use
the prompts in this chapter to journey
wherever your imagination takes you.

IMAGINATION STATION

Dream up a land where candy grows everywhere. Doodle what it would look like.

THINK LOLLIPOPS, LICORICE STICKS, COTTON CANDY, GUMBALLS, AND SALTWATER TAFFY!

Imagine a village where all the buildings are upside down. Draw that village here!

What is your favorite color? Draw a land where all the trees and plants are that color.

Dive into an orange ocean. What would the creatures look like in that imaginary sea?

ON SAFARI

Imagine traveling to the Serengeti plains in Africa for a chance to see animals (such as giraffes, elephants, zebras, lions, or antelope) in their natural habitat. What animals would you like to see? Doodle them here.

tHiS iS MY

_____

Name your country.

COUNTRY

Invent your own country
on the next few pages.

Doodle currency for your country.

Doodle/design a flag for your imaginary country.

65

Make a map of your country. What are the important landmarks?

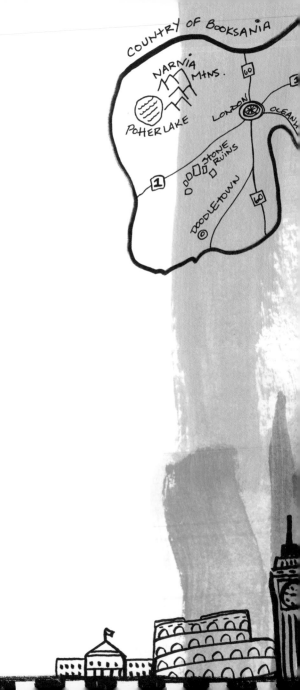

IT TAKES A

Design the town of your dreams. Where would the schools go? What about the town center, the baseball stadium, or the shopping mall?

VILLAGE

GleNN St.

FOREVER WAY

7th &
MAIN

SPRUCE

KNOTT's
RIDGE

REDLINE
Stop 2

StARS

Let's map out the subway system for your city.

GOING

UNDERGROUND

DRAW/COLLAGE A LAND
INSPIRED BY YOUR FAVORITE
BOOK OR IMAGINARY PLACE!

73

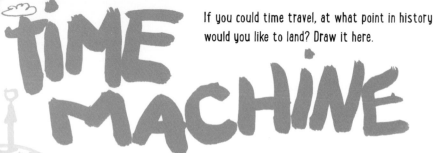

TIME MACHINE

If you could time travel, at what point in history would you like to land? Draw it here.

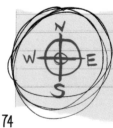

FOCUS ON ONE ASPECT OF YOUR CHOSEN TIME PERIOD, SUCH AS TRANSPORTATION OR CLOTHING: CARS FROM THE SEVENTIES, BIG HAIR OF THE EIGHTIES, OR NINETIES GRUNGE FASHION.

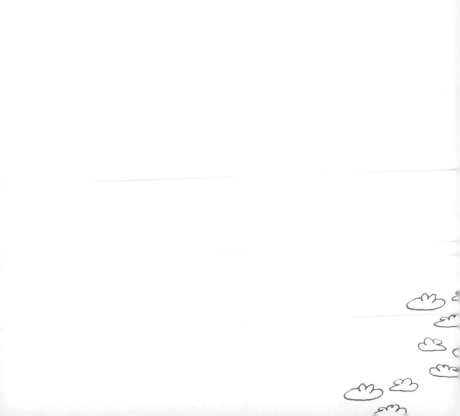

Imagine that you travel to another world. What would the beings look like? What about the surroundings or the spaceship you rode in?

ALIEN ADVENTURE

Where did you go in your dreams last night? Draw it here.

DREAMLINER

83

CREATE A
LAND OF
FUNNY
THINGS.

84

MAYBE THE MOUNTAINS ARE NOSES, THE PEOPLE LOOK LIKE CATS, AND THE CARS ARE SHAPED LIKE TOILETS.

ARTFUL AMUSEMENT

Imagine your own theme park. What would the rides look like? What would the attractions be?

Draw a map of your theme park.

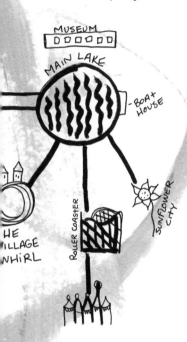

MUSEUM

MAIN LAKE

BOAT HOUSE

THE VILLAGE WHIRL

ROLLER COASTER

SUNFLOWER CITY

Doodle the tallest and wildest roller coaster you can envision!

OPPOSITES ATTRACT

Imagine a world that would be the complete opposite of where you live. What would it look like?

THE MORE WE
SEE OF THE
WORLD AROUND
US, THE MORE
WE LEARN ABOUT
OURSELVES.

CHAPTER 3

REAL JOURNEYS

FOR THE TRUE EXPLORER

Anytime you head somewhere else—school, the park, the library, the movie theater—you are taking a journey, which can turn into an adventure. Traveling doesn't always mean packing a large bag of clothing, getting on a plane, and landing in a completely different place. This chapter will introduce you to many prompts that you can apply to actual vacations or local jaunts. Keep an open mind, and your journeys will reward you!

THE WORLD AROUND YOU

What do you see right now? Doodle it here.

WHAT COLOR DO YOU
SEE MOST? DOODLE
WITH THAT COLOR!

PLACES IVE BEEN

Whether it's a trip to the zoo or maybe a journey across the country, document the places you've been with doodled symbols, writing, and photos.

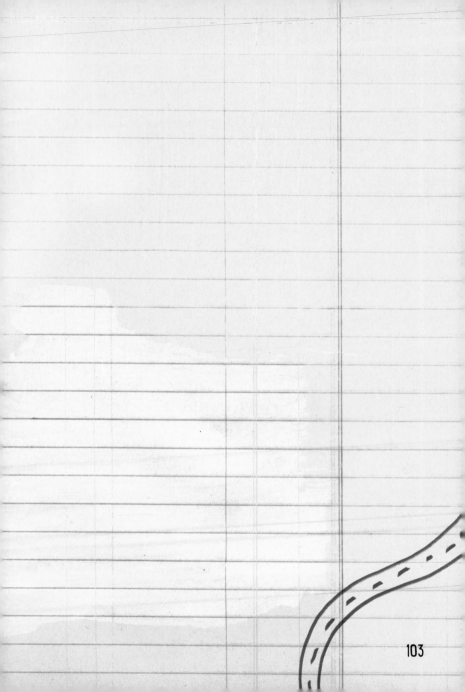

103

ON THE WATER

What would a boat journey be like? Doodle it.

DRAWINGS CAN BE AS SIMPLE AS FISH, WAVES, AND LIFE PRESERVERS.

SEEING STARS AND CLOUDS

Wherever you are, look up at the sky and doodle what you see. If it's nighttime, doodle the shapes you see the stars making. If it's daytime, doodle what you see in the clouds.

Doodle/collage images associated with trains and train travel.

OFF THE RAILS

OPEN YOUR MiND.
ADVENTURE is
ALL AROUND YOU.

LOOK AROUND YOU.

What colors do you see?
Color them in here.

112

Doodle world landmarks such as the White House, the Egyptian pyramids, the London Eye, or the Eiffel Tower.

ROAD TRIP

You're going on a road trip. What would you take with you?

A ROAD TRIP CAN BE ANY TRIP IN
A CAR, WHETHER YOU'RE GOING ON
VACATION OR TO SCHOOL. MAKE A
LIST AND/OR DOODLE THE ITEMS
YOU'D TAKE. WHAT THINGS WOULD
MAKE THE TRIP MORE FUN?

What do you see outside the car windows?

117

ROAD SIGNS

Doodle road signs and/or license plates you see while in the car.

"ARE WE
THERE YET?"

120

DOODLE THE WORLD.

DRAW BUILDINGS, HOUSES, TREES, AND OTHER STRUCTURES AROUND THE CIRCLE. ROTATE THE BOOK AS YOU DRAW TO MAKE IT EASIER.

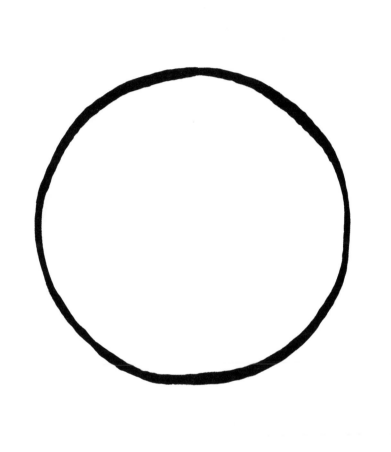

JOURNEY TO THE MOON

What would it look like?

125

Draw the faces of the people or animals you see while traveling.

DO YOU SEE IMAGINARY
FACES IN THESE SHAPES?
DRAW THEM, AS WELL!

127

129

Where in the world do you want to go? Make a list on the next four pages, leaving room for doodling after each destination. Doodle what you associate with that place.

132

135

You're taking a plane trip. Doodle what you see on the flight.

OKINO-TORI-SHIMA
PARECE VELA
(Japan)

Tropic of Cancer

LOOK OUT THE WINDOW
OF THE PLANE. WHAT
DO YOU SEE?

137

A TRAVEL PLAYLIST

What music will you or did you listen to on your trip?

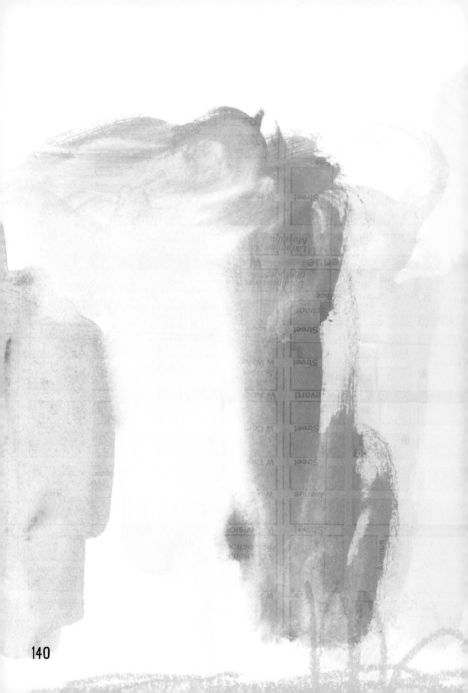

TRAVELERS ARE DREAMERS, ADVENTURERS, AND EXPLORERS.

Doodle the items you will take with you on your trip to _____

MAYBE IT'S A VACATION TO
AN AMUSEMENT PARK, GOING
CAMPING, A DAY TRIP TO SEE
YOUR GRANDPARENTS, OR A
VISIT TO THE LOCAL MUSEUM.

143

WAYWARD WALK

Venture out with your art kit and discover the world right around you. Whether it be your backyard or a nearby park, take some time to soak in your surroundings. Record the experience in doodles here.

WHAT SHAPES DO YOU SEE?
WHAT SMELLS ARE IN THE AIR?

Doodle items you took home with you from a recent adventure.

Add second line, hold it as you move a pencil

147

Collect things on your next trip. Fill these pages with tickets, receipts, stickers, and stuff you found on the ground. Either doodle them or tape or paste them down, and doodle scenes from your trip around them.

150

Make a map of a recent trip. Include landmarks and people you met there.

USE BITS OF PAPER TO
COLLAGE PARTS OF THE MAP.

WHERE DID YOU WANDER
TODAY? ANY EXCURSION
IS A JOURNEY!

THE VIEW

What do you see on your current journey?

What was the stinkiest or nicest smell you encountered on your trip?

Doodle the things you heard making noises on your journey.

USE ONLY THREE OF
THE COLORS YOU SAW ON
PAGES 112-113 TO DRAW
THESE THINGS.